MW00573195

A Special Gift

To

_____

From

_____

Date

_____

"*I didn't know what to do*"

Inspirational, idea-filled stories of caring people who chose to fight cancer together

by Sara Sabalka

"I DIDN'T KNOW WHAT TO DO"
Inspirational, idea-filled stories of caring people
who chose to fight cancer together
Copyright © 2001 by What-2-Do Publishing
All rights reserved

Published by:
WHAT-2-DO PUBLISHING
8601 F-5 West Cross Drive, #222
Littleton, CO 80123
866- 259-6700 (toll-free)
sabalka@aol.com
www.what-2-do.com

Manufactured (printed and bound) in the United States
10 9 8 7 6 5 4 3 2 1

compiled by Sara Sabalka
with
Dwight Andrew and Karen Baer

Cover Photography by Scot Henderson

Library of Congress Cataloging-in-Publication Data
Sabalka, Sara
 I didn't know what to do: inspirational stories of caring people who
chose to fight cancer together / by Sara Sabalka with Dwight Andrew
and Karen Baer.
  p. cm.
 ISBN 0-9707499-0-2 (pbk.)
 1. Inspiration. 2. Love. I. What-2-Do Publishing. II. Sabalka, Sara.
 III. Title. IV. What-2-Do.
 Library of Congress #2001090580

No part of this book may be reproduced in any form, mechanical or electronic, without express written permission from the publisher, except by a reviewer who may quote brief passages in a critical article or review to be published in a magazine, newspaper, newsletter, website or other periodical.

Acknowledgments

This page could be a book in itself. There have been so many "angels" that have made this project come to life. My family has been more than just supportive. Without the working commitment from Dwight and Karen, these pages would still be on my computer. Chelsa, Chad, and Chase have helped their mom take a dream and make it a reality. A big hug goes to my loving mother, who, through her unconditional love of my dying father for six years, taught me how to encourage and inspire those who are facing adversity. I love ya mom!

Also, a special thanks to Gail Coors, a fellow survivor, who challenged me to compile these stories and write this book, and whose personal story, "A Rose of Hope," (p. 18) inspires me every time I read it.

Finally, a special thanks to the many other people who were willing to share their experiences, both good and bad, of how their family and friends reacted to that most life-changing news, "You've got cancer." Many of the contributors to this book asked to remain anonymous so that the spotlight would be on the story. Therefore, the names of the contributors have not been included.

To underscore my commitment to fighting breast cancer through research and education, I will be donating a portion of the proceeds from book sales to cancer charities.

Dedicated to the
memory of my dad, Tom
and to cancer patients
everywhere who are
struggling for their very
lives against this disease,
and to those family and
friends who want to
provide them hope,
encouragement and
love— to people who
want to know
what to do.

He answered:

"'Love the Lord your God with
all your heart and with all your soul
and with all your strength
and with all your mind'; and,
'Love your neighbor as yourself.'"

Luke 10:27 (NIV)

Contents

Contents
(continued)

My Story

I Didn't Know What To Do

I still remember the look on my mother's face when I walked into that faded yellow hospital room. My father was lying there in a white, sterile bed where he had been for the past week. I knew instantly that something was wrong . . . really wrong.

My father had just been told that he had a rare form of bone cancer and that he had only six months to live. In effect, he'd just been given a death sentence. But little did these doctors know about my dad's inner strength. He fought every day for more than seven years before he finally succumbed to this horrific disease.

Probably the most difficult part of his struggle was that he had to do it without the support of some lifelong friends. I would see these people in the grocery store picking up something for dinner, on a family picnic in the park or on Sunday mornings at church. They would usually be very polite and ask, "How's your dad doing?"

I was always ready with a courteous update, but wanted instead to say, "Why don't you just call him and ask?" They would usually end our conversation with this awful resignation, "We just don't know what to do."

I wanted to scream, *"Do anything! Just do something!"* I know that their comments were well-intentioned and that they really did care about my dad. The problem was that they really didn't know what to do.

Maybe this experience with my dad is why, in 1990 after my

gynecologist told me she found a lump in my breast, I didn't share the news with anyone except my husband and mother. I didn't want anyone to know, because I was afraid that they wouldn't call either.

When the lump started to grow, I immediately scheduled a biopsy. My 45-minute biopsy turned into a three-hour partial mastectomy. I awoke from the anesthesia and felt like a truck had driven over my chest. Little did I know, I was about to embark on a new chapter in my life.

I went home to a long and very private recovery. As I laid in bed with a bag of frozen peas on my chest, I thought a lot about the significance of why this would happen to a young woman. I had never dreamed it would happen to me (I know; we all say this), because I didn't have even one of the known risk factors. But I knew there had to be a reason.

About three weeks into my recovery, the reason became clear to me. I realized that if I shared my personal experience with other women, a life might be saved and needless anguish and pain averted. I vowed to make this my mission.

Much attention is paid to women 50 years and over regarding breast cancer, but less concern is typically paid to younger women—those in their 20s, 30s and 40s. According to statistics published by the American Cancer Society, nearly one quarter of all breast cancer cases occur in the younger age bracket. For this reason, I wanted to let young women know about the reality of breast cancer. Even if you're a *young* woman, you *are* at risk for breast cancer.

But to get my message across, I needed a "door-opener." It came when I was crowned Ms. Colorado USA. No surprise—my platform for this "beauty pageant" was to educate girls, women, and men about breast cancer. And, believe it or not, my on-stage question was: "Is your *cup* half-empty or half-full?" It was a really ironic question and I didn't know quite how to respond. So, having recently endured a partial mastectomy, I said, "Both."

Through all the speaking engagements before and after that event, something wonderful began to happen. I was learning the true meaning of friendship. Survivors were coming up to me and sharing stories of love and encouragement they'd experienced during their recoveries. I'm not talking about just receiving meals or cards (which are certainly thoughtful), but heartwarming, going-out-of-their-way, downright creative ways of how their friends helped them in a time of need.

I can't tell you how encouraged I was by the many stories I heard. However, I did know that if these stories encouraged me, they could certainly encourage others. So I started collecting the stories and have compiled them into this book. I want to share these stories, and ones I've not yet heard, so they can be an inspiration to the friends and family of loved ones who are facing a difficult or even deadly disease such as breast cancer.

Another thing happened along the way. When my website went online, I tragically received many stories and notes from people who said that no one was there for them. Not family. Not friends. No one. More than once, the ink from my printer became illegible as my tears fell to the page.

One such note came from Lisa: "I wish I could say that there were a lot of supportive people around me when I was sick, but there really weren't. It seems that people really don't know how to behave around people with a serious illness. I worked full time while I was undergoing chemo. My chemo treatment was every other Friday and I would leave work at about noon to head over to the cancer center. One day as I was preparing to leave, a co-worker said, 'Well, it must be nice to have the rest of the day off.' As if to say that I was going to do something enjoyable for the rest of the day by being hooked up to an I.V. and getting poison injected into my veins."

Another survivor, David, wrote: "My fight against cancer was pretty much a 'do-it-yourself' project.... My best friend just couldn't handle my illness and other friends were certain I was dying and didn't know what to say."

It's my hope that no one should ever have to hear a friend say, "*I didn't know what to do.*"

*Never
tell people how
to do things,
tell them what
to do and they
will surprise
you with their
integrity.*

-George Patton-

Your
Stories

A Rose of Hope

It was March of 1991, and I was about to begin my nine dreaded treatments of chemotherapy. The afternoon before the first treatment, my sister-in-law, Sharna, showed up at the house for an unexpected visit. When I opened the door, she was standing there with a bouquet of nine crimson-colored roses. Of course, I was pleasantly surprised, but couldn't have anticipated the positive impact these flowers would have.

Sharna explained to me that this bouquet was the first of nine that I would be receiving. I was thrilled to learn that she would bring me flowers after each of my chemo treatments. A month later following my next treatment, Sharna came to visit again. And as promised, she held out a bouquet of nine roses. But this time, only eight were red. The ninth rose was snow white.

After each subsequent treatment, my sister-in-law arrived just like clockwork with one less crimson rose and one more white one. Her visits continued through September, when she gave me the last bouquet. It was literally breathtaking to see nothing but nine white roses. I felt that both a physical and spiritual cleansing had taken place and remember thinking: "Look how clean I am!" Our tears of joy only magnified that experience.

The visual image was much more dramatic than I could have expected. With each treatment, bad cells were being invisibly cleansed from my body and replaced with healthy ones. But to be able to lie there and actually *see* the change through these simple, yet beautiful, surrogates was more encouraging than I can adequately describe. As I neared the end of my chemo treatments, I found myself looking forward with increasing anticipation to coming home, where I would receive my bouquet with one more white rose.

A Velvet Heart

I was diagnosed with breast cancer in 1998. I had never been so scared in all my life. Within the last five years I had watched my Dad, my first husband, and two brothers-in-law die from cancer. I underwent both a lumpectomy and lymph node removal, followed by seven weeks of radiation.

The one to hear my fears and walk with me through all of it was Tina, my sister-in-law. She would come to my house to bathe me, change my dressings, clean the house and cook. She took me to all of my doctors' visits. And somehow, she was able to do all this while working and caring for her own four young children.

So when testing a year later showed another spot in the same breast, the first person I called was Tina. She was there, all over again, for moral support as well as hands-on help. This time my treatment was radical—a complete mastectomy. I discovered a new level of fear as I not only worried about my life and my recovery, I also worried about my "wholeness" with one breast gone.

Tina understood as only a woman and a dear friend could. As I was prepped and waiting for the surgery, Tina handed me a huge gift bag stuffed with bright pink tissues. Inside was a big white teddy bear—the floppy, soft kind that molds to your body regardless how you hold it. Tied around its neck was a pink ribbon and a tag which read: "Hold me close and I'll hug your heart." I smiled and squeezed Tina's hand, thinking her gift was just like her, thoughtful and sweet. Before I was wheeled into the operating room we named her "Lovey."

Once I was out of recovery, Tina handed me a gift-wrapped box. Inside was a bright pink tote bag with a picture of a big white teddy bear on the front and the words "Hugs inside, please take one and call me whenever." She explained that this was the carrier for my new teddy bear. I could use it to carry not only Lovey, but all the little things I would want (like lotion, a notepad and pen, some lemon drops) when I went for chemo treatments.

When I walked with my rolling IV pole down the hospital hallway the next day, many people commented on the decoration hanging from the side bar: a bright pink bag with a smiling white bear poking her head out. I told them who she was and what she was for. The day I was released, Tina arrived to help. As we prepared to leave the room, she handed me a pink velvet heart with the name "Lovey" delicately stitched in the center. Tina told me she sewed it on so Lovey's heart could be seen by all.

Lovey became my constant companion for the next few months. I carried her from room to room during my recovery, and to all of the doctor and hospital visits for follow-up testing and treatment. When anyone would ask about her, I'd tell about my sister-in-law and then invite Lovey to give them a hug, too. She always brought a smile with the hug, especially for kids.

Lovey still travels with me whenever I go out of town. And people always want to know the story behind the well-loved white bear with the pink velvet heart. I tell them she's my best friend, my sister-in-law, in disguise.

We make
a living by
what we get.
We make a
life by what
we give.

- Winston Churchill -

All Wrapped in Love

I've got a great story about what my co-workers did for me!
The story began when I was told that I needed a stem cell transplant. I worked in the emergency room at a hospital and Janice, a
nurse friend of mine, was the instigator.

Janice was a pretty "craftsy" lady and had run across a pattern
for a signature quilt in one of her sewing books. So she decided
to make one for me. She cut out squares of white fabric, then
hand-delivered or mailed the pieces to many of my current and
former co-workers—some of the doctors, nurses, and other staff
I'd worked with during my twenty-three years at the hospital.

She asked them to create a short note or symbol of encouragement on the fabric. Some wrote me loving messages, others drew
pictures, and some created poetry. These were a few of my
favorites:

> A spiral-shaped note from my supervisor, Susan:
> "you can do it … you can do it … you can do it …
> you can do it" with a flower at the end of the words
> and her name below.

> A handprint from Mike, an equipment technician,
> with the names of his family members written on
> each finger.

> A pink velvet heart sewn in the middle surrounded
> by the words: "May you feel our love every hour of

every day, Mandy & Steve"—a fellow nurse and her husband.

A clever poem: "My gift to you, this little square; A symbol of the times we've shared; We've worked real hard—we've laughed some, too; But lots of work we've yet to do! So mind your doc and get well quick; If not I think *I'll* end up sick!—Dr. Nick".

And from Janice herself: Every other border square was bright pink with a quilt-print heart sewn in the middle and signed "Made with love, Janice"— 24 of them total!

Janice incorporated these signature pieces, along with colored accent fabric, into a lovely quilt and presented it to me a couple of days before I was admitted to a major Boston area hospital for surgery. In addition to the quilt, she gave me a "get well soon" card. It read, "When you wrap this quilt around you, you'll be surrounded by our love and well wishes."

I used the quilt constantly while hospitalized and then again when I returned home to complete my recovery. On cold winter days, I still use my signature quilt to wrap myself in their love . . . and it still brings tears to my eyes!

Angels Next Door

My elementary-age boys and I had moved to Arizona when my business in Tulsa went under, leaving me nearly broke. Phoenix seemed to be an area ripe with opportunities in the industry I knew best—microcircuitry. We had lived in Phoenix for only about a month when I found out through a routine physical required by a potential employer that I had testicular cancer. No family history, no warning signs. It devastated me. I felt so alone, and I was in many ways, since I had no friends or family in the area. To make matters worse, the company opted not to hire me.

Fortunately, I carried my own insurance and still had coverage for most of our medical bills. But money was rapidly running out and, being laid up, I had no idea how we were going to pay for such basics as food or rent. That's when my landlords—our next-door neighbors and honest-to-goodness angels—came to the rescue.

Charlie and Doris were a retired couple who had owned the duplex for twenty-seven years. I told them about my situation and need to delay upcoming rent payments. They had a lot of sympathy for me because Doris had lost a brother to prostate cancer three years earlier. They told me not to worry about rent until after I had completed my recovery and was able to look for a job again. With that load off my mind, I underwent the pre-surgical tests.

My parents arrived from Oklahoma the next week. The day after they arrived, Charlie and Doris came over with two bags of groceries and an offer to help in any way if my parents couldn't stay through my entire recovery. They had already met the boys and seemed to get along fine, so I graciously accepted their offer (and the kind gift of food).

Charlie and/or Doris stopped over daily, bringing fresh-baked goodies, and little gifts for the boys or just helping around the house. They also spent time with my parents, chatting and playing card games. Once, when two of their school-age grand-children were visiting from across town, they invited us over for an evening of Monopoly. Twice a week they arrived with another bag of groceries. They said they'd mentioned my situation in their Sunday School class and others wanted to help. By the day of my surgery, Charlie and Doris had become like second parents to me and were called "Papa" and "Nana" by my boys.

Their care continued when I was hospitalized. They visited me daily, bringing over food to the house and spending time with my parents and the boys. I'd been home recovering for a week when my parents had to fly back to Oklahoma. At that point, Charlie and Doris became my life line. They'd stop in each morning to get the boys ready for school. After school, the boys would often spend time with them while I rested. They were also there when I was lonely or discouraged. Two months after my surgery, I found a job and was able to pay the rent again, including the three missing months. But "Nana" and "Papa" insisted that the missed rent was their gift to me.

Three years later, I'm still cancer free. My life has changed a lot, but two things remain the same: Charlie and Doris are still "Papa" and "Nana" to the boys and they are still guardian angels to me. I can't imagine how I'd have made it without them!

Butch 'n Buster

I was devastated the day my CAT scan showed the lymphatic cancer I had battled two years before was probably back. To keep my mind off the biopsy scheduled for the next day, I asked my daughter Ginger to come over and help me organize my study, something I'd been wanting to do for months. With my wife's passing away the previous October, I needed Ginger's help tackling the huge stack of photos and memorabilia my wife and I had collected over our twenty-eight years together.

The three big cardboard boxes were slowly being converted into scrapbooks, when an old, slightly torn Polaroid photo slipped onto the floor by my knee. I picked it up gently, remembering how special this picture was.

"Butch," I said, as if that explained everything. Realizing this meant nothing to Ginger, I continued. "My dog when I was about your age. I'd just moved here from Minnesota and didn't know anyone. Back then, I worked at the old shoe factory across town. I hated coming home to an empty place each night. So I got Butch. He was just a puppy and I had to teach him everything, but he was great! Every evening when I'd come home, he'd be patiently sitting on the sofa by the door. I took him camping, to the park each Sunday, and I even took him to the local drive-in theater to see *Lassie*. He was the best!"

I slowly sighed, thinking about happier times, then wiped a tear from the corner of my eye and placed the photo in its sleeve. As we finished working that afternoon, I continued to reminisce while my daughter listened.

Early the next day, Ginger drove me to the hospital, lending me emotional strength as we waited for surgery. Hours later, on the drive home, I was pretty quiet, already dreading the next few months' difficulties. As I opened the front door, I was greeted by a quiet yip and a rough tongue on my hand.

"What's this? Whose dog is in my house?" I exclaimed, confused and a little alarmed. I bent down to calm his initial reaction to us. He was a young, fairly frisky spaniel—about the same size as Butch had been.

"Dad," my daughter half-whispered from behind me, "He's *your* dog if you want him. He's about two years old and completely trained. I picked him up this morning from the animal shelter. I just thought you might like some company..."

Before she could finish I turned around, wrapped her in a big bear hug and whispered in her ear, "I think I'll call him 'Buster.'"

Buster and I became almost inseparable. When I was home recovering from chemotherapy, Buster would quietly follow me through the house, resting his head on my foot when I sat down. And Ginger often laughed when I would start a sentence with "I was telling Buster just the other day..." Ginger's thoughtfulness, in the form of my four-legged companion, was very special. Three years later, I'm now fully recovered, and Buster and I are friends for life.

Don't walk
behind me;
I may not lead.
Don't walk
in front of me;
I may not follow.
Just walk beside
me and be
my friend.

- Albert Camus -

Can Do!

I'm writing this story to help others understand how much it means to have children involved in a cancer patient's recovery. I work at an elementary school in rural Alabama and was stricken with ovarian cancer in early fall.

Anyone, male or female, can certainly use a little extra income when faced with cancer. With all of the tests, treatments, doctor's visits, and medicines, the financial burden is staggering! It's very difficult to ask friends or family for money, even when it's really needed. Oh, I could ask for help with simple things like a meal or occasional childcare, but I just couldn't ask for money to pay my bills while I wasn't able to work.

You can't imagine how touched I was when I heard that the school was organizing a fundraiser—not for new books or equipment, but for me! I assumed that their efforts might include a car wash (or two), a bake sale, selling candy door-to-door, or something simple like that.

Instead, my co-workers decided to have the children do something even more basic—just collect donations directly on my behalf. In art class, the kids made collection cans out of empty coffee cans, pasting my picture on one side with the phrase "Can Do!" on the other. They decorated the rest of the can to their own individual tastes. After school, they solicited family, friends, neighbors, and employees of nearby businesses to donate just one quarter. I'm sure that the children knew they were helping me. But I think their real encouragement came from the male staff at the school, all of whom agreed to have their heads shaved if the kids could collect $5,000 in just one month. I never would have thought that such a small act could be such a *big* incentive, but it certainly was!

It took them only *two weeks* to reach the goal! I had no idea what was going to take place when I was asked to come to the school for a "surprise." When I got there, all the students and faculty were assembled in the gymnasium. A small stage was located at one end of the gym and on it a large, clear plastic water barrel bearing the slogan *"Can Do!"* sat alone.

The principal began by thanking everyone for participating in the fund-raiser. He then asked each student, class by class, to come forward, deposit their quarters in the barrel and place their can on the stage to form a pyramid. When the last donation was presented, he announced how successful the fund-raising effort had been: more than $5,200 had been collected! I was overwhelmed! I tried to hold back the tears, but failed miserably, as I stepped forward to thank them.

For the grand finale, the twelve male teachers who'd been the kid's motivation came forward, each followed by a female teacher wearing a big grin. Then, with an "on your mark, get set, go!" and a simultaneous roar from the kids, the razors started up. To the kids' delight (and I must say, mine, as well), all twelve men had their heads shaved right down to the scalp. It was so much fun for the children and so touching for me. I'll remember their generosity and enthusiasm forever!

Circle of Friends

Waiting on lab results is the hardest part. When you know there's nothing you can do but wait, the fear of the unknown can almost be paralyzing. That's the way I felt about the follow-up appointment for my lumpectomy. The appointment with my doctor was scheduled for 10:30 A.M. and I had a very bad feeling about the results. At 9:30, the doorbell rang and I opened the door to find my friend, Joan, standing there with a well-worn Bible in her hand. With just a glance, she could tell I was nothing but a bundle of nerves.

"I'm sure you're anxious about your biopsy and I'd like to pray for you, if that's okay," she offered.

"Okay?" I responded. "That would be wonderful." I invited Joan into the living room and offered her a cup of coffee. As she began to pray, I felt a sense of peace come over me. It's hard to describe, but it was sort of like curling up in a nice warm blanket that's just been taken out of the dryer on a cold winter's day.

"Ding, dong." The doorbell chimes snapped us out of our prayer. Another friend, Stacey, was standing on the front porch, also clutching a Bible. "Mind if I join you?" she asked, seeing Joan seated in the background.

"Sure. There's plenty of room. Come on in." About five minutes passed and the doorbell rang again. And again, one of my friends was ready to join us in prayer. So it went. About every five minutes, another friend joined us to the point where I just left the front door open, so that they could let themselves in.

When the time came for me to leave, six very dear friends had formed a circle around me, hand in hand. They ended our time together by reading one verse each of Psalm 23.

"The Lord is my shepherd ..."
"He makes me lie down ..."
"He restores my soul ..."
"Even though I walk through the valley ..."
"You prepare a table before me ..."
"Surely goodness and love will follow me ..."

"Amen." How incredible! The love and strength that my friends gave me was more than I could have imagined. Their support was what enabled me to cope with the dreaded diagnosis of breast cancer and gave me the strength to endure the difficult treatment program that lay ahead. I knew that with God's help, through my circle of friends, I was ready for the fight.

Eight chemo treatments and eight "prayer circles" later, I was pronounced cancer-free! What a joy and blessing my friends are!

Hand-in-Hand

I had been having "dizzy spells" off and on for a month or two. The last episode was classified a seizure and happened while I was driving. Fortunately, I was going slow and the car simply wandered to the side of the lightly traveled road before stopping.

The doctors were extremely worried about me and immediately rushed me to a large hospital in nearby Des Moines, where I was placed in intensive care. The final diagnosis was a small brain tumor. Surgery was almost immediate. At the spry age of 79, I was told I would have a long recovery, including radiation treatments.

My daughter, Debbie, lived nearby and was an almost daily visitor while I was hospitalized. She and her husband were my moral support. Debbie was also the one who kept the rest of my family informed, including my granddaughter, Karrie, who lived in Colorado with her husband and two young daughters.

The day of the surgery I slept almost nonstop. Early the next morning, I woke from my anesthetic haze to find an amazing sight hanging beyond the end of my bed. It was a string of fourteen brightly colored paper dolls joined hand-in-hand and stretching almost from one wall to the other. Just then, Debbie poked her head into the room. When she saw that I was awake, she came on in.

She smiled when she saw I was admiring the paper dolls, then sat down next to me holding a big envelope. Inside the envelope was a letter from Karrie. Her letter wished me well and told me she and her daughters had wanted to do something special to support me from 700 miles away. I looked back up at the dolls. They were all custom decorated, some with lacy dresses, others with stripes or polka dots. The three in the middle had the names "Karrie," "Kristy," and "Jessie" written on them. The two "girls" even had the bright yellow hair of my two great-granddaughters.

Not only did these happy faces greet me each time I woke up for the next two weeks, but they were a big hit with the hospital staff, too (I had more than one nurse stop by my room just to see them). Debbie took a picture of my room, showing the dolls hanging above the many floral gifts. She mailed Karrie a copy of that picture, as well as one of me waving to the camera from my hospital bed.

I like to think those simple dolls holding hands with each other symbolized Karrie's family—make that my entire family— holding my hands as I struggled through my recovery period. One year later, the three center dolls still hang in my bedroom as an ongoing reminder of my family's love and support from hundreds of miles away.

I am only one;
but still I am one.
I cannot do
everything,
but still I can do
something;
I will not refuse
to do something
I can do.

- Helen Keller -

Hat Day

My son, Jason, had been fighting stage 2 leukemia for a month when the chemotherapy treatments began to affect his hair. Within a week, he went from being a full-headed blonde to a mostly bald child. The big problem wasn't the treatments themselves, but Jason's feelings of being different. As he put it, "I'm the only kid in my whole school who is bald. The kids don't really tease me, but I can tell they are staring at my head."

I knew I had to do something, since our elementary school had a strict policy prohibiting hats' being worn inside the school building—anytime for any reason. I understood the need to keep any possible gang apparel out of the school, but Jason's situation was considerably different.

I contacted the principal and asked if Jason could be exempted from the hat policy. He agreed and suggested a wonderful solution—Hat Day. Not only was Jason allowed to wear a logo-free hat every day, but each Friday through the duration of his chemo treatment all the kids in the school were allowed to wear a logo-free hat in support of Jason. For the privilege of wearing a hat in the school building, each child was asked to give a donation of $1.00 to the PTA.

By the second week, a local screen printer had volunteered to design and print bright blue and pink kids' baseball caps at no cost. Each cap was imprinted with "I'm a Friend!" and was sold by the PTA to children in the school and to the community for $5 per hat. The support was amazing. We even saw a group of pre-

schoolers at the zoo one afternoon adorned in pink and blue
"Jason hats." We found out later the daycare teacher was the
mother of one of Jason's classmates. Jason went from being
"different" to being a celebrity within our community. His
feelings of being an outcast vanished.

At the end of the ninth week, an assembly was held in the
school gymnasium. Our entire family attended. Everyone wore
a hat. The donations from Hat Day and from selling "I'm a
Friend!" hats had been combined, and we received a check from
the PTA for $3,382!

We had been told about this assembly in advance and our
family made a poster-sized card that we presented to the school.
It read:

> To all the students and faculty of Cedar Ridge
> Elementary from Jason Willis and his entire family:
> You have lovingly given of yourselves in this time
> of family crisis and we gladly count you as
> "Friends of Jason." Your care is beyond words,
> so we simply say . . ."Thank you" from the bottom
> of our hearts.

Our hand-signed card, a picture of Jason with a big smile
on his face and a brief narrative are now displayed next to the
school office in a framed glass case. They are a testimony to the
spirit of love and support from that school to our son, a fellow
student in need.

Hats and More Hats

Two weeks after I began my chemotherapy for breast cancer, my hair started to fall out. Before I began chemo I had to make the decision about whether to buy a wig or to wear hats. I decided that it was more my style to wear a hat, even though I hadn't really worn hats earlier in my life. For several days I thought about buying some hats, but I was in denial and just couldn't bring myself to do it.

My father was in town to help with the kids during all of the tests that came right after diagnosis. The night before he left, he insisted that I get out the American Cancer Society catalog and order as many hats as I wanted. It was his and Mom's gift to me. The hats arrived a week later, and they were wonderful. My favorite one was a denim floral hat. It made me feel very chic!

For me, wearing a hat became a symbol of healing. It meant that I was on my way to beating the cancer, that I could continue my normal life while fighting the disease. So, when I received a straw hat from my in-laws, I knew they understood what I was facing and believed in me.

Later, my neighbor and her 6-year-old daughter bought two bandanas for me. One was bright pink and was perfect for the Race for the Cure I eventually ran in. The other had bright yellow happy faces all over it. What a delight!

And then, as winter approached, a friend and her daughters brought me two chenille hats. Until then, all my hats were summer hats, so it was really nice to have warm hats to wear on chilly days.

By including their daughters in these gifts, my friends were teaching their girls a little about breast cancer, chemotherapy, survival, encouraging one another, and getting on with life. Hopefully these girls will have learned that there is no shame in surviving cancer. You can hold your head high, even when it has no hair!

Do all the
good you can,
by all the means
you can, in all
the ways you can,
in all the places
you can, to all the
people you can,
as long as
ever you can.

- John Wesley -

I'm Going with You

My friend Marita is a go-getter, a real dynamo. When I told her about my diagnosis of breast cancer, she reacted just as I expected her to. She hugged me, shed a quick tear with me and then said, "Let me help you!"

We got together about a week after our first conversation. She handed me a heavy tote bag and explained that inside was information about all kinds of things to help cancer patients. I love Marita's energy and enthusiasm, but at that moment I wanted to hand her back the bag and tell her to go home. I was depressed, sleeping poorly, and generally crabby. The last thing I wanted was a pep talk.

That was my first reaction. But as Marita opened the bag (while I sat in total silence) and began explaining what was inside, I couldn't help but listen. Immediately after I had told her my situation, she had done some serious research of her own, calling and visiting the oncology unit at a nearby hospital, the American Cancer Society, the Komen Foundation, and her health club. Marita's question to all of them was: "What support activities and groups do you have for someone going through cancer treatment?"

Marita had not only gathered brochures, schedules, and even one short video, but she had organized the material into these categories:

Cancer support groups—what they do, when and where

Activities specifically for cancer patients—both
one-time events and ongoing activities

Information sources—everything from national
cancer hotlines to good websites

Some of the information in her bag included a breast cancer
support group schedule, a free one-year membership for breast
cancer patients at the health club, an American Cancer Society
catalog with adorable wigs and hats, hospital-sponsored education class list, and even information on an annual catered dinner
for breast cancer survivors.

After reviewing all the possibilities, Marita leaned forward,
waiting for my comments. When I just laughed at her diligence
and energy, she pulled my calendar off the wall and asked,
"What shall we write down? And remember, wherever you go,
I'm going with you."

Before Marita left she had written two items on my calendar
(and two on hers also). Before my treatment was completed, I
had attended just about everything she had mentioned that first
day. Just getting up and going made all the difference, and
knowing I wouldn't be doing any of it alone was a huge encouragement. She was my motivation at a time when I had little of
my own.

It Is a Joke

When I was diagnosed with cancer, my daughters were 4 and 8 years old. My older daughter, Veronica, was active in a neighborhood Brownie troop. When they discovered my plight, her Brownie troop put together a beautiful notebook containing all the Scouts' favorite jokes and riddles. In addition, they got many of my neighbors to contribute their favorite stories and jokes as well.

The twenty-five pages of this book included mostly silly, frankly even stupid, jokes. But the humor and lightheartedness of these children is what made it so special. A few of my favorites were:

Question: "Why was the duck so sad?"
Answer: "Because his *bill* was in the mail."

Question: "What has three feet, but can't walk?"
Answer: "A yardstick."

Question: "How many men does it take to screw in a light bulb?"
Answer: "Three—one to replace the bulb and two to brag about it!"

On the cover page, they wrote, "Lisa, we hope this brings a smile to your face, a laugh to your belly, and warmth to your soul. We want you to know you have a whole neighborhood of support and that's no joke!"

This little book brought me much laughter—to the point of tears. And, at that point in my life, happy tears had been hard to come by. Sometimes laughter really *is* the best medicine.

The only gift is a portion of thyself.

- Ralph Waldo Emerson -

It's for the Birds

The first thing you notice is how weightless they are. You see, the effects of a mastectomy are many, but the one that caught me by surprise is the change in mass. For about thirty years, my body had grown very accustomed to the weight of my breast tissue. A diagnosis of stage 4 breast cancer and two complete mastectomies changed all that.

After the surgery, I was given temporary prostheses at the hospital that were pretty realistic, as far as the size and shape was concerned. The prostheses were hollow, fabric forms stuffed with cotton for support. When concealed beneath my hospital gown, they allowed me to look normal. However, they just didn't *feel* normal.

Early in my recuperation, I was lying in bed at home watching cardinals, blue jays and the ever present sparrows at a feeder outside my window. As I watched them, I had an odd notion. Why not replace the cotton in my temporary prosthesis with birdseed? It would be much closer to the right weight and firmer than the cotton.

I immediately called my husband, Steve, who was on his way home from work and asked him to go buy some more birdseed. I didn't tell him why and he went way overboard— two 10-pound bags! I guess he just wanted to make sure that I'd have lots of birds to watch. He had no idea what I had in mind for that seed. Later that evening I removed the cotton, filled both prostheses with birdseed and sewed them closed. They were just the right weight and molded perfectly into my bra.

One of my first ventures out of the house was to the surgeon's office for a post-surgical check-up. After the nurse took Steve and me into the examining room, she left and we were alone. To be prepared for the doctor, I took my bra off like I usually do, but, without thinking, didn't take the prostheses out first. They fell straight to the floor. Unfortunately, I guess I hadn't sewn them up very tightly. Both pouches exploded on impact, sending birdseed everywhere as we exploded in laughter!

At the same instant, my doctor knocked on the door. I quickly leaned against it so he couldn't come in—laughing hysterically the whole time. He must have thought the cancer had knocked me off my rocker. Meanwhile, Steve was on all fours, trying futilely to gather up the birdseed. It was s-o-o-o comical! Steve did the best he could, but he didn't even come close to getting all of it.

When I finally let the doctor in, we both had tears streaming down our faces. His first step inside crushed some of the rogue birdseed. He looked down and exclaimed, "I'm so embarrassed. This room really needs sweeping." At that, Steve and I both burst into laughter again and the tears ran. My doctor just kept saying, "Don't worry. You will get through this." To this day, he doesn't know how the bird-seed got there. But what amazes me is that this story is still making the rounds in local support groups some eight years later!

Just a Heartbeep Away

I used to disdain those little black boxes. You know, those little electronic beepers that always seem to go off at the most inopportune times: like the final scene of an elementary school play; or the middle of a crucial business meeting; or worse yet, the conclusion of a pastor's sermon, just as the benediction is about to begin. Sure, they're great communication tools, but pagers just don't have any respect for the privacy of the receiver. At least, that's how I used to feel.

That was before my doctor uttered those fateful words, "You've got breast cancer." Like most cancer patients, I was devastated by the news. I was especially downhearted when he said that it was inoperable and that I would need chemotherapy. I knew I was literally in the fight of my life, and I felt so alone.

But then my church learned of my plight and it seemed everyone wanted to get involved in my cancer battle. They told me they didn't want to bother me by constantly calling and asking how I was doing, but wanted me to know that they cared. So they got me a beeper.

The beeper number was given out to the whole congregation and they were encouraged to call that number whenever they were thinking of me or praying for me. The congregation was also kept abreast of my schedule for key activities, such as doctor's appointments or chemo treatments. The results were incredible!

My beeper was going off all the time, especially during doctor's appointments and chemo treatments. At those times, the pages were almost non-stop. The doctors and nurses were amazed at how many people were thinking of me at that very moment (and so was I!).

I could read the phone numbers and often know who had beeped me. Many times, however, I received pages from people I'd never met. The wholly unconditional nature of those beeps was particularly special to me.

I never would have guessed that this little communication tool would be such a tremendous boost to me and play such a great role in my recovery. Knowing the prayers of family, friends, and even strangers were just a heart*beep* away was a wonderful encouragement!

The habit of
giving only enhances
the desire to give.

- Walt Whitman -

Just Say It!

During the week after my first-ever mammogram and subsequent diagnosis of breast cancer, I called many family members and friends to let them know what was going on. For me, each phone call was a little therapeutic.

When I called our friends Bob and Susie to tell them my news, Bob answered the phone and we had a long talk. We talked about Susie's father's long fight with cancer, and then he said something that shook me to my core. He simply said, "We love you."

It had been more than fifteen years since I'd heard those words from someone who wasn't a close family member. But I knew he meant it, and I knew exactly what he meant. He meant the same thing that so many people have shown me, although no one else was as direct. But whenever someone brought dinner to my family when I was exhausted from chemotherapy, I heard Bob's voice in my head saying, "We love you." And with every note, letter, gift, and phone call, I heard his voice yet again. When my neighbors made me promise to call them if ever I needed anything, I heard what they were really saying.

Here are some of the specific things people did that said "We love you":

> Collected money from my friends and neighbors
> to pay for a cleaning service
> Took me to the Race for the Cure and made a
> pledge on my behalf (one of my neighbors canvassed
> our neighborhood gathering donations!)

Gave me a cute hat—it wasn't expensive or
bizarre, but very practical
Made me the kind of dinner I like in disposable containers (turkey dinner with trimmings
and potato soup were my two favorites)
Gave me books—on nutrition, alternative health
care, religion, and jokes
Came to a treatment with me when my husband
was out of town
Brought me fresh fruit—after my surgery I was
so nauseous that I could hardly eat, but fresh
apple slices were just the ticket
Sent lots and lots of cards and flowers—these
were always treasured

The greatest gift I received from my two cancerous tumors
was the open expression of love from those around me. With
surprising honesty and depth people began saying, and showing
me, "I love you." The next time something horribly scary
happens to someone you love, tell them "I love you." Use those
words often.

Life Goes On!

I was a 35-year-old mother with a 6-year-old son and a 4-year-old daughter when I was diagnosed with breast cancer. It seemed never-ending, the twelve weeks of chemotherapy, a lumpectomy and follow-up radiation treatments. During this time I found myself trying to hang on to my life as I had known it, but much of each day was spent dealing with my disease.

There was one very bright moment, a first break in the heaviness of those weeks. Just after I was diagnosed, my friend Jill stopped by on a Saturday morning to see if I wanted to go to an art fair with her. Having two young children, I rarely did anything spontaneous and had never been to an art fair. It just didn't fit my schedule or my children's interests.

My husband said he'd stay with the kids, so off Jill and I went. We spent two hours wandering aimlessly through row upon row of artists' creations, with no goal in mind except just "being there." We chuckled at some of the most outrageous sculptures we'd ever seen and openly admired the beautiful watercolor landscapes of another artist. It was relaxing, freeing, and simply fun to feel alive and think about something besides breast cancer.

I continued to seek out fun activities throughout my treatments thanks to Jill's leading. We took a trip to Florida, visited the local amusement park, took hikes in the mountains, and more. Friends were often amazed that I felt well enough to do these things, but I felt it was so important to continue living and having fun as long as I had the strength.

Thank you, Jill, for starting me down the road and helping me embrace an active, full life—even in the midst of strenuous cancer treatments. I will always treasure your thoughtfulness.

Making the Grade

Being a high school teacher, I often had days when I wondered if I was having any impact at all on the teenagers who were in my classes. Were they ever going to get past the raging hormones and grow up? My experience has been that if you teach long enough, you find they do mature and most grow up wonderfully, at that. Mary was just such a person.

I remembered Mary from my tenth grade Government class. She was a sweet girl with lots of friends and, as I recall, she was above average academically. Now, twenty-four years later, it seemed a little odd to be meeting with her at the first parent-teacher conference of the school year. Her oldest daughter, Jamie, was a sophomore in my Political Science class. We discussed Jamie's performance to date (no problems there) and spent the remainder of the conference just catching up. When time ran out, we decided to continue our conversation over lunch the following week. One thing led to another, and by January we were getting together pretty regularly for coffee on Saturday mornings. Although we hadn't planned it that way, Mary and I were fast becoming good friends.

When I noticed symptoms that prompted a colonoscopy in March, Mary was the one who listened to my fears. She took me to my test and was the one who held my hand when the doctor told me I had cancer. She also held my mother's hand when I told my parents the diagnosis. And Mary spent the first night at the hospital with me after my surgery, so that my elderly parents could get some rest.

She was by my side through the entire ordeal, taking me to almost all of my chemotherapy treatments. And Mary's entire family jumped right in to help, too, including her parents, her younger daughter and, of course, Jamie. They provided meals and helped keep my house clean. Most touching of all to me was Mary's care for Whiskers, a young horse that I'd owned for about two years—my "family" since my husband had died four years earlier. Mary took Whiskers to her acreage and cared for him so I wouldn't have any worries. She fed him every morning, brushed his coat every week, and occasionally rewarded him with carrots and apples. I think that horse ended up even more spoiled than he was before.

I will be forever grateful to Mary and her family for being there every step of my way. They were amazing—pitching in and taking on whatever needed to be done. They not only did my "homework," but turned in tons of "extra credit" as well.

As a teacher, I was used to being the one in charge, the one with the answers, the one helping others. Through my cancer and Mary's help, I learned that amazing things can happen when roles are reversed. She taught me what true love and friendship are all about. In the most important class—Life 101 (Love and Care)—I give Mary an A+!

My Special Ally

I was diagnosed with lung cancer back in 1998. At first I was scared, then depressed, and finally angry. I was also confused. I was told I would have to have the upper lobe of my right lung surgically removed. Although my family and friends were supportive, I think they were just as confused as I was. I was filled with questions about the surgery, my recovery, long-term implications, etc. It seemed like I was in a battle zone, and I didn't know who to turn to.

My first step in getting answers to my many questions was to go on the Internet and try to find out as much as I could about my specific form of cancer and the treatments. At one site, I found personal stories about survivors' individual fights against cancer. One story, coincidentally, was written by someone whose cancer was in the same location as mine, and was being treated at the same cancer center that I was. Her surgery had been successful and her checkups were showing no return of the cancer. Luckily, at the bottom of her story, this woman had left her e-mail address.

That's how I met Barbara. I quickly e-mailed her and asked whether she would mind answering some questions about the surgery and recovery. Almost immediately, she e-mailed back, saying she would answer all my questions; I only had to ask. We constantly e-mailed back and forth. Barbara answered my questions about the surgery (of which I was extremely fearful) and told me about the hospital stay. Peace and confidence returned to me a little bit more with each e-mail she sent.

Barbara also put me on the prayer list at her church. I started receiving "prayer-grams" in the mail from people I didn't even know, saying such things as "I'm praying for you," "You and Barbara are both in my prayers," even "I lift your situation up in prayer each morning." Each of those messages gave me courage and strength. With all of the prayers and support from Barbara and her friends, I was at peace as they wheeled me into the operating room.

The operation went smoothly, and my recovery was fairly short. During those weeks, I continued my e-mail contact with Barbara. I can honestly say I don't know if I could have done it without her help. Although I had the full support and prayers of my family, it certainly helped to had have a person who'd been through it guide me along the way.

I had my one month follow-up the day after she had her one year follow-up, both at the same hospital. We just missed each other. My oncologist—let me rephrase that—"our" oncologist told me there was no evidence of cancer on my X-ray. I learned from Barbara afterward that her results were the same.

I have never personally met Barbara nor even spoken to her on the phone. Yet she is now a dear friend, a true ally in my fight against cancer. Thanks, Barbara! You blazed the trail for me and then shared your experiences freely so that I could confidently face this enemy—and win!

Too often we underestimate the power of a touch, a smile, a kind word, a listening ear, an honest compliment, or the smallest act of caring, all of which have the potential to turn a life around.

- Leo Buscaglia -

Net Working

Kids don't get cancer. They get ear infections or strep throat, but they don't get cancer. Old people do. At least that's what I thought until our son, Jonathan, was diagnosed with a rare form of leukemia at the age of 13.

Jon's treatment program periodically left him too weak to stay in touch with his friends. Like many youngsters, he had many good friends and enjoyed talking with them over the telephone about the really important issues—homework, pop music, and the latest fashion trends. His reduced ability to communicate with those friends brought on a depression of sorts.

About a month into his treatments, I mentioned Jon's lack of social interaction and its effect on his psyche to one of my friends. My concerns touched Robin in a way I didn't expect, but for which I'm most grateful. I guess I shouldn't have been surprised, because her son was one of the friends who had drifted away from Jon.

Robin was a programmer for a major software company, but she also dabbled in website design on the side. About two weeks after we talked, she invited me over to her house for coffee and told me that she had something she'd like me to take a look at. Robin took me into her office, logged on to the Internet, and went to "Jon's Site."

Jon's Site was wonderful! Robin had designed it with two goals in mind: (1) to provide updates on Jon's treatments and progress, and (2) to enable Jon to conveniently communicate with his friends. The banner, "Jon's Site," was framed in footballs (his favorite sport) and included a kicked football flying through a bright yellow goalpost. Jon's smiling face adorned the home page and the menu buttons included:

"Scorecard" ("Results of my latest treatments")
"Game Plan" ("My future treatments")
"Scouting Report" ("Info on this form of cancer")
"Training Camp" ("What I need to beat this")
"Film Room" ("What am I supposed to study?")
"Chalk Talk" ("Let's chat about things")

Not only did Jon's friends regularly visit the site, his teachers did too and used it to keep him updated on schoolwork.

Through "Jon's Site," he also heard from other kids in similar situations, as well as from some of their doctors and nurses. Thanks to Robin, being a part of Jon's world was as easy as "point and click."

One Step at a Time

That first morning came very early, 6:00 a.m. to be exact. I wasn't sure I could do it, but said I'd give it a try. I still remember that morning in June like it was yesterday. The sky was clear, except for a few thin clouds on the eastern horizon. In Colorado, that makes for some glorious sunrises, and this was certainly one of them. I felt so alive and was glad that my friend Jeannie had encouraged me to join her on her morning walk.

A week or so earlier, I had been diagnosed with breast cancer, and Jeannie had found out about it. She was determined to see me through my illness and was convinced that physical activity would benefit me greatly. So even on those mornings shortly after a chemo treatment, when I could only make it a block or two, she never complained. She'd just offer me a couple of lemon drops and we'd turn around and head home, knowing that there were better days to come. And there were. So on those few days when my husband had to meet her at the door and tell her I wasn't able to go at all, she never got discouraged. She always came back.

These walks were very therapeutic for me. My body was betraying me, but I was still able to make it work. It not only worked, but actually grew stronger as the days went by. As my body was strengthened, so was my mind. I became mentally tough and knew that I could endure this difficulty—whatever the outcome. Walking with Jeannie gave me a feeling of independence and life that I so badly needed.

My last chemo treatment was administered exactly three weeks before the local Race for the Cure. Through Jeannie's unwavering dedication and support, I walked the 5K course in that event. Only this time, I did it on my own with a pink race card pinned to my back that said, *"In Celebration of . . . Me!"*

*In the middle
of difficulty lies
opportunity.*

- Albert Einstein -

Only a Call Away

I'm a survivor of breast cancer. During the entire period from diagnosis to completion of chemotherapy I was blessed with a very special neighbor, Jan. My husband and I were overwhelmed. We were trying to educate ourselves on cancer treatment options, as well as reorganizing our family schedules to maintain a minimal sense of normalcy in our household for our two young daughters.

The thought of dealing with all the people who wanted to help was more than we could handle. I didn't want to turn anyone away, and that's when Jan volunteered to intercept all the calls from people who wanted to bring food or help in some other way. Her organizational skills were amazing. I would let her know what our specific needs were and she would consult her list of people who had offered to help. On my chemo nights, and the night after, when I was still feeling bad, someone would promptly be at my door with a delicious meal. I didn't have to do a thing.

Jan also coordinated with those who wished to help in other ways, from cleaning my home every other week to shuttling my girls to various activities. It was as simple as calling her to tell her of my needs. I truly treasured all the help, but would never have called someone myself to ask them to do many of those things. And if Jan didn't hear from me every few days, she would call to find out if there was anything I needed. For everyone involved it seemed easier and safer to have a "middleman." She also could give those interested an update on how I was doing, eliminating any anxiety they might have about asking me directly.

Every few weeks Jan would supply me with a list of everyone who had contributed meals or something else. That way, it was easier for me to return dishes and write thank-you notes. She was so organized she even kept track of the well-wishing calls and passed along their comments, too.

Could I have survived without Jan? Yes. Would I have maintained my sanity without her? I sincerely doubt it.

Out for a Joy Ride

For me, the hardest part of recovering from breast cancer surgery was the seemingly endless hours spent lying in bed. I was such an active person before, and watching time tick by was very difficult to accept. My mind kept going full speed, even when my body couldn't. Before long, the days all ran together and I lost my sense of time.

Three weeks into my recovery, my husband, Jeff, called me around lunchtime and told me that he had a little surprise for me that night and that we'd be "going out." I begged him to leave me at home, because I didn't have the strength or the desire to go out in public yet. I had no hair or energy and still felt a little nauseous. But he insisted and then told me I could just stay in my bathrobe. That last part me really confused me. Go out—in a bathrobe?

I napped for several hours and managed to find enough energy to get ready. At 6 p.m., Jeff walked into our bedroom carrying a dozen long stem red roses draped over his arm like a beauty pageant contestant. He laid them across my lap and handed me an envelope. As I opened the envelope, it dawned on me that today was our sixteenth wedding anniversary. I'd completely forgotten about it!

"Are you ready to go?" Jeff asked. "I suppose, but where are we going?" I responded. A big grin and a "you'll see" was all he gave me for an answer.

We started down the stairs, but I wasn't even sure I could make it on my own. Suddenly, all I wanted to do was to go back to my safe haven under the covers. How on earth was I going to go out for the evening? I think he must have heard my thoughts because, like Richard Gere in *An Officer and a Gentleman*, he gently scooped me up in his arms and carried me out the front door.

Waiting there for us at the curb was a white stretch limousine with a driver standing by the open rear door. As Jeff set me carefully inside, I could see that he'd used pillows to convert one of the long bench seats into a bed for me. The indirect "mood lights" were turned down and created a warm glow inside. My favorite Kenny G album was playing softly as Jeff poured some ginger ale into a tall champagne glass for me. It was very nice.

"Okay, where are we going?" I asked again, even more worried than before about the answer. "Oh, nowhere special. We're just for going out for a little joy ride." With that, he instructed our driver to take us around the town. As we rode, Jeff served me a five course dinner (way more than I could eat) that he'd ordered as take-out from our favorite restaurant.

Although I'd been very apprehensive, I was thrilled now to be out of the house and looking at something other than the four overly familiar walls of our bedroom. As the evening progressed, I felt more energetic than I had in a long time. In fact, time passed so quickly, it seemed like our three-hour trip to nowhere had taken only a few minutes. It was great to focus on something other than my cancer, and Jeff's anniversary gift to me was a real "joy ride."

Paris in Springtime

My name is Chris and, right after my 35th birthday, I was diagnosed with breast cancer. My whole life I had always eaten right and exercised, and I had no family history of breast cancer. Besides, I always thought that it happened to someone else and not someone young like me.

I'm sure there's literally no good time to get cancer. But for me, this time was the worst. It was mid-April and months earlier I'd made plans for a vacation to France. I'd never been to Paris before and had specifically arranged a springtime visit so that I could see it all abloom with flowers. My departure was scheduled for May 13th, only now my mastectomy was scheduled for the same date.

My very best friend, Jennifer, knew how excited I was about taking this trip. She'd been to Paris several times and had been very helpful with suggestions on which sites (and shops) to visit. As she relived her trips, I think she was almost as disappointed as I was that my trip would have to be canceled. I couldn't have anticipated the "trip" she had planned for me.

She offered to keep watch on my place while I was in the hospital and drove me home when the doctors said I could go. It was May 15th, but rather than visiting the Louvre, all I felt like visiting was my bedroom. The term "blue" was a gross understatement of how I felt.

She unlocked my door and helped me up the stairs to my bedroom. The door to my bedroom swung open and, surprise of surprises, I *was* in Paris! I was greeted by several miniature Eiffel towers, each adorned with little white lights and a pink ribbon on top. Jenny had also visited a local travel agent and picked up half a dozen posters of Paris, which replaced the artwork that used to hang on my walls. And flowers were everywhere! The floral arrangements I'd received in the hospital, and several new ones from Jenny, adorned my bedroom. The room was as fragrant as a perfume factory.

As soon as she got me situated in bed, Jennifer hit the "play" button on the VCR and a travel video of Paris began. Jennifer paused the tape only a moment later and exclaimed, "Oops, I forgot something. I'll be right back." She returned with a bottle of chilled champagne (non-alcoholic, due to my medications), two crystal wine glasses, and an assortment of the most decadent French pastries and chocolates that you've ever seen.

Although I knew Paris was eight time zones away, I felt like I'd just been transported to the Champs Elysées. I knew then that I was on the road to recovery. After four years and three real-life trips to Paris, I still cherish this memory and Jenny's kindness. And it still amazes me that something so simple could virtually catapult me to another continent and have such a positive impact. Thanks, Jenny!

*I have found
the paradox that
if I love until
it hurts, then there
is no hurt, but only
more love.*

- Mother Teresa -

Pillow Buddy

I distinctly remember the day I told my best friend, Becky, I was going to have a lump in my left breast removed. It was the day before her 40th birthday and the day before my surgery. We cried; she spoke words of encouragement; and then we even laughed about the rotten timing. We had plans to get away the next weekend to a nearby resort for lots of fun and relaxation without any work or children.

My husband, Roger, was with me the day of the surgery, while my three children were at school. We arrived home shortly before the kids did and I went right upstairs to bed. Although I was exhausted, I couldn't sleep. My back ached if I lay flat on it and I couldn't lie on either side—having no support for my chest or lower body hurt too much.

My frustration and pain had led to tears by dinnertime. I remember snapping at Roger when he came up to ask if I wanted anything to eat. It was then that the doorbell rang. Roger answered the door and I heard the voices of Becky and her two young children. My husband peeked into the room and asked if I felt like company.

"Yes," I sighed. "Maybe they'll help me forget about how uncomfortable I am for a little while."

I heard giggling and paper rustling as they climbed the stairs. When they walked in, they were holding a big package wrapped in bright giftwrap. Because of the way they carried it, I could tell it contained something soft. After a quick squeeze of my hand, Becky motioned for her kids to bring the package over to me.

Roger held the gift up so that I could unwrap it myself.

Inside was a 5-foot-long "body pillow" brightly decorated with spirals, squiggles, smiley faces, hearts, and all the artists' names. But the best design on the whole pillow was on the top where they had made a large face with big eyes, a crooked nose, two cute ears, and a grinning mouth. They had even finished their masterpiece with some yarn, dark brown like Roger's hair, and glued it on with a hot glue gun.

Roger and I had oohed and ahhed at the decorations, but when we saw the "face" we couldn't help laughing out loud. It hurt to laugh, but it still felt good inside. "This is too funny," I grinned. "The doctor told me I'll just want to lie around for a few days. But I guess I won't be hanging out alone. And I really need something to support my body." I gave Becky and each of the kids a big squeeze with my right hand.

I did indeed hang out with my "pillow buddy" for many days. Without it, I don't know how I'd have survived being in bed for so long. And even now, it "lives" in my bedroom on the easy chair (when it's not being borrowed by one of the kids or propped up in bed when Roger is away on business).

Queens of Hearts

Tuesday mornings at 9:00 A.M. was when we got down to business. Our husbands were off to work, the kids were off to school, and a fresh pot of coffee had just finished brewing. Time for a couple decks of playing cards and the Tuesday morning bridge club. I know it sounds a little old-fashioned, but this weekly card game was something that the eight of us thoroughly enjoyed. Coffee, croissants, cards, and camaraderie—life was good!

I never dreamed how much I would treasure these friends until I was told that I had colon cancer. In March of 1998, I began noticing the symptoms and arranged for tests early the following month. When the results came back, I was told that I needed surgery right away and that I would be laid up rehabilitating for several months thereafter.

As I thought about the upcoming months, I was pretty scared and anxious about how successful the treatment would be, and how my family and friends would react. I was particularly concerned about how my bridge club would react and didn't know how to tell them about my situation. Because I'm an avid gardener, I was also concerned about whether my physical condition would force me to miss the spring planting season.

Two weeks before surgery, I finally mustered the strength to tell the club about my impending operation. Instead of pulling away, as I had feared, they became wonderfully supportive. Our card parties were suspended out of necessity, but all of them visited me during my hospital stay and brought me beautiful floral gifts.

Not cut flowers, but potted ones that could be planted and enjoyed later at home. Each of the pots was labeled with the name of a bridge partner—Anne, Denise, Michelle, Cynthia, Sandy, Connie, and Stacey.

When I returned home from the hospital, I had a huge surprise waiting for me. Knowing that I had a long and difficult recuperation ahead, my card club had gone to our local nursery and purchased a variety of bedding plants, seeds, and bulbs. On one of the Tuesdays while I was lying in a hospital bed, they got together as usual at my house, but with trowels rather than cards.

When I returned home, I was greeted by my flowerbeds planted full of petunias, pansies, mums, roses, and irises. They looked spectacular and, having tended these beds for years, I knew how much time and effort my club had invested. However, one small flower bed next to the front door was noticeably void of flowers. Instead, seven signs were planted in that flower bed — each with the same directions and an arrow pointing down to the soil: "Plant me here, Love, Anne"; "Plant me here, Love, Denise"; and so on. The signs had been carefully arranged so that the plants complemented one another perfectly.

The following Tuesday, I still wasn't strong enough to play bridge. But I was able to join my club on the front step to watch them each plant their final gift of flowers, the ones they'd given me in the hospital. For the rest of the summer, every time I went in or out our front door, I was reminded of these seven special ladies—my "Queens of Hearts." And, yes, we still get together every Tuesday for another round of cards, coffee, and camaraderie.

The greatest
mistake you can
make in life is
to be continually
fearing that you
will make one

- Ellen Hubbard -

Ready, and——Action

I had been told for years that the enlargement of my uterus was most likely due to fibroid tumors. It wasn't until a tumor manifested itself by growing outside of the cervix that the correct diagnosis was made—cervical adenocarcinoma stage 2b—not exactly the news I'd been hoping to hear.

What followed was five weeks of external radiation and two separate hospitals stays for internal radioactive implant treatments. With all that radiation, I figured I'd glow in the dark. In fact, visiting time in the hospital was limited to just one hour per day, because of radiation exposure to visitors. But that wasn't the worst part.

The worst part was that kids weren't allowed to visit at all. I have three kids who, at the time, were 14, 10, and 6 years old. The hospital was about two hours from my family and friends. While I missed them greatly, I told everyone that I really didn't want them to drive such a long distance only to be able to visit for an hour.

My husband, Mike, completely ignored my directions, however—just as I knew he would. My kids, on the other hand, came up with an ingenious way to "visit." Sarah, my eldest and most creative child, decided that if that I couldn't come home to see them and they couldn't visit me, then the only viable alternative was for them to bring home to me.

Both times that I was away Sarah used our family's video camera to record home life. She sent the camera and tape with Mike for me to watch, and then borrowed a neighbor's camera to continue filming while I had our camera at the hospital. Each time he visited, Bob would arrive with a new cassette about thirty minutes in length and take with him a short video of me to share with everyone at home.

Sarah chose not to film many "staged" events. Instead, she filmed our typical, everyday life and added her own narration along the way. I got to see a little of Ben, my youngest, practicing his saxophone. I think he felt really pressured by the camera, because he had considerably more squeaks than normal. She also filmed Jack in the street out in front of our house, trying to flip his skateboard with his feet and land on top of it. Sometimes, I was afraid that he'd end up needing to be hospitalized too, or at least put in a foot cast when he didn't quite land it right—which was most of the time.

I also got to see the kids playing ball in the backyard with Spanky, our peekapoo puppy, and Mike mowing the lawn. When Mom stopped by to bring over dinner, Sarah filmed the whole thing, including close-ups of each dish. I couldn't smell them, but her chicken casserole and fresh green beans looked a whole lot better than the hospital food I was eating at the time.

I know the events Sarah taped don't seem like much. None of them were particularly noteworthy. But as I lay in a hospital bed in a faraway city, they meant the world to me. Those tapes kept me in touch with my family when I needed them most. Their love, strength, and support was the best treatment of all.

School Spirit

I was teaching English in a public high school when I was
diagnosed with cancer. Being an older, single woman, I was very
unsure about how I could weather the financial difficulties of
being unable to work during the spring semester. I was just as
concerned about how I would cope with the emotional challenges
that lay ahead. I couldn't have imagined the help I would receive.

At the next weekly staff meeting, teachers throughout the school
voluntarily decided to donate their own sick leave to replenish
my rapidly diminishing leave. Most teachers contributed one or
two days. But Betty, another English teacher, went beyond the call
of duty and gave me more than a week of her precious time off.
I felt a heavy burden lifted as they each shared their sick leave
with me. At that point, I knew I would be able to get paid throughout the entire semester because of their generous gifts.

My next thought was how I was going to survive the rigors
of surgery and chemotherapy, both physically and emotionally.
Again, my colleagues came through. Although a neighbor took
me to most of my chemo treatments, she was sometimes unavail-
able. When she couldn't, the school librarian, Vicky, and the principal, Richard, were there to get me where I needed to be. And
they always did so with tons of encouraging words and lots of
hugs. To support me and help me remember the overwhelming
amount of information, one of the three went with me to each
and every one of my doctor's appointments.

The head of our department, Anita, kept in touch with me

almost daily, taking me out to lunch when I had good days. And Betty taught not only her own classes, but mine as well, so that the kids would get all their lessons. Finally, one of the math teachers, Ernesto, took over my duties as student council sponsor. He attended council meetings, reviewed and approved council decisions, and even oversaw planning of the annual spring student council event, "Visit the Schools," where ten nearby universities were invited to be part of an education fair.

My students were wonderful, too. They were all so encouraging to me as soon as they found out about my illness. Many e-mailed me and stayed in touch throughout the semester. I often received get-well cards written by the class, some even showcasing their blossoming literary skills.

While there is no good time to get cancer, I discovered a wonderful place to be when the diagnosis came—teaching school. The staff and students gave me something to hold on to during some of the bleakest days of my life—gifts of time, love, encouragement, and even sick leave.

I'm now back to full speed, but it seems somehow the school changed in my absence. The smiles seem brighter, the words of encouragement more real. The days even go by more rapidly. I can still feel the love and support I knew for so many months. It's a new "school spirit" that will always live for me in these halls.

Something Old...

My first round of chemotherapy treatments was no big deal. I had anticipated that it would really knock me down, but it didn't. No sickness, no hair loss, no problems. I actually felt pretty normal and was able to continue my life with very few changes. Most important, I was able to help my daughter with all the plans for her upcoming wedding.

Since it was the first wedding for any of our three children, we went to great pains to ensure that it would be perfect. It had always been a dream of mine to sew my daughter's wedding dress. I started the project right on schedule and had allowed plenty of time to finish it. But when the doctors decided that I needed a second round of chemo, everything changed. This time the drugs made me very sick and lethargic. I could barely get my strength up to eat and bathe. My dream of seeing her in that gown was fading with each passing day.

I got so sick that my three neighbors started bringing us meals. In the process, they noticed that the dress on the dining room table was not showing any progress. They knew the big day was getting closer and how very important that gown was to my daughter and me.

I think it was on Friday just one month before the big day that my husband came into our bedroom where I was resting and asked if I was up for some visitors. I said, "I suppose," and the next thing I knew, my room was filled with my neighbors and their sewing equipment. While my husband went downstairs to get the gown, they told me, "We're here to help you finish the job."

For the next three weeks, we spent an hour or two together each day to further the masterpiece along. Early on, about all I could do was offer a little advice on the alterations and nod quiet approval of their efforts. But as the days went by, I began to regain my strength enough to help with the sewing. When the gown was finally finished, it turned out better than I had ever dreamed of. In fact, it was perfect!

The wedding day finally came and, with tears streaming down my cheeks, I watched my daughter being escorted down the aisle by her dad. Her gorgeous white train trailed gently behind them. My first thought was how lucky I was my cancer had been found early enough for me to witness this event. My next thought was how symbolic the gown had become to all of us. It wasn't just a labor of love from me to her, but a symbol of my friends' love for me.

*Now join your
hands, and with your
hands, your hearts.*

- William Shakespeare -

The Business of Caring

My bout with breast cancer came when I was 42 and the marketing manager for a software firm in Illinois. It was a dream job for me. As a part of the company's marketing department for the past fifteen years, I traveled a lot and had attended many industry conventions and trade shows, both as trade show exhibitor and seminar speaker. I also worked closely with our twenty-nine sales representatives within the United States and Canada and met many of our clients.

When I was told one rainy October morning that my right breast would need to be removed, I was, for probably the first time in my life, speechless. And so was my boss, Charles, our vice president of marketing. He was supportive and encouraging, but asked only as much as he could sense I was ready to share. I knew that I couldn't keep up with everything and we agreed that I would turn all of my short-term projects over to our three marketing support personnel while I concentrated on the pending surgery and the inevitable long recovery.

My last contact with the company before the surgery was at our annual sales meeting. All the sales reps, marketing staff, and top executives of the firm met for four days, not only to talk business, but to foster an environment of teamwork. At the wrap-up session, I was asked to join my boss and the president at the podium. Then all the marketing staff walked in with a 6-foot-high poster in the shape of a computer terminal. The large print said, "You can do it, Donette! We're all on your side!" And written in a stunning variety of colors were more than 335 signatures of people I knew through my numerous industry activities. Many wrote words of encouragement as well. One of our fiercest rivals had boldly written just three words—"You go, girl!"

After I recovered from the surprise, Charles explained that at the industry's largest convention the prior week (which I had been unable to attend due to pre-op tests), they had posted the "card" at our exhibitor's booth. A simple sign had been attached explaining that I was not attending this year because I was battling breast cancer. The staff manning the booth had worn badges stating "For Donette" with a looping pink ribbon glued onto the front.

That card was so comforting to me I requested it be placed in my hospital room so I could see it when I awoke from surgery. Charles stopped by each of the eight days I was hospitalized. He would always point to that card and say, "Gotta get back. Look at all the people who miss you."

Then when I arrived home, I was stunned by another showing of love from those I worked with, also instigated by Charles. Each sales rep had purchased an oversized get well card and had gathered more signatures from clients I had met during my many years. I think those totaled another 145 names. A third set of cards came from each department in the company itself, adding another 124 names to my collection.

I had expected help, support, and love from my family and friends. And I received that in vast quantities. But the gifts of a few words from people I knew in the "working world" were completely unexpected. I wouldn't trade their support, competitors or not, for anything.

The Card's in the Mail

Life was pretty normal. I was approaching the upper end of "thirty something" with a wonderful husband and three young sons. Invasive ductal carcinoma (i.e., breast cancer) simply wasn't on my "To Do" list—neither were three related surgeries, six months of chemotherapy and five-and-a-half years of medication.

The diagnosis took me completely by surprise. Actually, it took our small town by surprise, too. In a small town, any local news generally travels fast, and it didn't take long before most folks knew of my diagnosis. I must say that it brought out the best in my neighbors. Shortly thereafter, I got numerous cards and flowers, and even quite a few phone calls from friends who offered their assistance.

One particular card came in the mail on Friday, two days after my mastectomy. It was a pretty typical get-well card with some flowers and a nice poem, but what caught my eye was the signature. The words below Maurine's name indicated she was my neighbor's mother. Maurine was a lady I'd met only on rare occasion and really didn't know very well. I made a quick mental note of it, because I'd never expected to receive a card from someone so far removed from me.

The following week, I got some more cards, but they diminished in numbers rather quickly. On Friday, the mailman came and, to my surprise, I got another card from Maurine. The card was similar to the first with a few key words underlined. Two cards in two weeks seemed rather special.

Then came week three and with it a third card from Maurine. By this time, I was receiving only an occasional "thinking-of-you" card. I really cherished this third card, and the hope and support it offered.

My treatments continued without interruption for the next six months. The cards didn't, however—with one notable exception—Maurine's. I didn't despise those people who didn't send additional cards, but rather looked forward with increasing anticipation to Friday's mail and Maurine's card. When chemo knocked me down, her cards were always there to pick me up.

It was a simple, little thing—just a card in the mail. But for seven straight months, Maurine's cards kept me going. A card or two is ordinary, but twenty-eight cards are extraordinary. Thank you, Maurine!

Faith
makes all things possible.
Love
makes all things easy.
Hope
makes all things work.

- Unknown -

The Chemo Pack

It was an unusual gift. But then, it was an unusual time in my life, too, and in that context the gift made perfect sense. You see, I was struggling with something that I'd never experienced before—chemotherapy for treatment of breast cancer. At the time, I felt as if my world was crumbling around me; physically, emotionally, and spiritually. But the gift helped me through it all.

When I began my chemotherapy treatment, a group of women, whom I knew from PTA, came to my rescue. On one of my first treatments, Elise and Rhonda, two women in this group, picked me up to go to the hospital and gave me that wonderful gift. The gift was a clear plastic backpack on which they had painted "Lisa's Travel Bag" in bold letters. The backpack was filled with lots of little "goodies," including magazines, playing cards, notepad, pencil, hand sanitizer, flavored lip gloss and bottled water.

This "chemo pack," as they referred to it, was a simple, but precious, gift indeed. For its comforting qualities went far beyond its physical contents. This gift made me feel cared for and supported. My friends had looked beyond my medical predicament and sought to meet my personal needs.

When you begin chemotherapy, you're generally told about the side effects. But you don't usually get much simple, practical instruction on how to deal with them. In addition to the previous items, I found the following useful and have since given these chemo packs to several women facing similar circumstances. I trust that you will find these ideas useful, too. And be sure to personalize this gift with a few of your own special items. After all, it *is* the thought that counts.

> To help neutralize the horrible metallic aftertaste
> of chemotherapy ...
>> A large tin of strong peppermint lozenges
>> and a bag of lemon drops
> To pamper skin that gets so fragile ...
>> A large bottle of bubble bath and an assort-
>> ment of fragrant lotions
> To help quiet a nauseous stomach ...
>> A box of crackers
> For the inevitable constipation ...
>> A bag of prunes
> To reduce the discomfort caused by bleeding gums
> and mouth sores …
>> A bottle of non-alcohol mouthwash, tooth-
>> brush, and a tube of toothpaste

And last but not least, for the perpetual runny nose and the many tears that are shed, several travel-size packages of tissue. I opened the last package when I was told my treatment had been a success!

The Great Shave-Off

It's a well-known fact that one of the first things we notice about one other from a distance is our hair. So when it's missing, completely missing, particularly on a young or middle-aged person, we sit up and take notice. For that reason, a lot of people noticed our son, Brian.

Brian had been diagnosed with a rare form of bone cancer. His doctors had recommended an aggressive treatment program that included strong doses of chemotherapy. Hair loss was one of the inevitable side effects and ironically became a symbol of support.

Brian's dad, Jim, was a police dispatcher. Law enforcement agencies are known for being close-knit groups and the police department in our Colorado town was no exception. Jim's co-workers wanted to show their support for Brian by doing something special, so they organized "The Great Shave-Off."

Two special officers, Randy and Adam, put the whole thing together. They contacted a nearby hair salon asking if the stylists would be willing to donate their services for the shavings. The owner not only agreed to donate their services, but offered to contribute their standard fee of $10 per haircut to a related cancer charity. Randy and Adam also called a local blood bank asking if they could be on site to take blood donations as well and, of course, they enthusiastically agreed.

At the appointed morning roll call, a number of public servants happily volunteered to have their heads shaved. Two female officers even stepped up to have their locks removed in support of Brian. Rather than getting a "freebie," each participant still gladly paid for the haircut, so that each shaving effectively became a $20 donation, thanks to the matching funds from the salon owner. In all, 62 heads were shaved, $1,240 was raised, and approximately 50 units of blood were donated.

This outward expression of support for our son was obviously what caught everyone's attention. For many of the citizens of our community, the sight of bald police officers prompted many curious stares and brought back memories of Kojak sucking on a lollipop. But to our Brian, The Great Shave-Off demonstrated loudly and clearly how much his dad's co-workers cared.

The Green Room

It was a pretty typical 2,000 square foot, two-story house in suburban Fort Worth. Thanks to the prior owner's neglect, it was also a fixer-upper. But we were determined to make it our "new" home. With the help of my best friend, Susan, and her husband, we gave the house almost a complete makeover.

But we just couldn't quite do it all before the time came to move in and our master bedroom ended up getting shortchanged in the process. It had sickly green walls that were downright depressing. They constantly reminded me of another time and place; one that was buried somewhere back in the early '70s, right next to lava lamps and pet rocks. In fact, the "green room" became the subject of quite a bit of friendly ribbing between Susan and me.

But my bedroom was just about the last thing on my mind as I got the unexpected news that I had breast cancer. At that point, I became totally absorbed in my treatment program, which included a double mastectomy and eventually chemotherapy.

During my hospital stay for the mastectomies, Susan came and visited me every day. Her visits were a real encouragement and, I'm sure, accelerated my release. I should say, however, that she visited me *almost* every day, because on the day I was released she was noticeably absent.

My disappointment vanished, however, when I saw Susan's car parked in my driveway. She had come over to welcome me home. We gently hugged, and I told her how happy I was to see her and how *excited* I was to go the "green room" to recuperate.

As she escorted me down the hallway to the bedroom, I recall telling her that I thought I smelled fresh paint. Susan just smiled and opened the door.

The sickly green walls of my bedroom were nowhere to be found. They had been replaced by pure, ivory white walls and a beautiful floral border of yellow roses. Susan had also replaced the sun-faded curtains with matching drapes. And our ratty old bedspread was nowhere to be found. It had been exchanged for a whole new set of matching linens.

I was stunned for a minute and forgot completely about what I'd just been through. I tried to say something, but couldn't manage a single word. Neither could she. So we just stood there and gently hugged again. We let our tears of friendship say it all.

Thanks so much, Sue! You definitely colored my world with your love.

*Coming together
is beginning,
keeping together
is progress,
working together
is success.*

- Henry Ford -

The Radiant Eight

After my lumpectomy was done and my lymph nodes had been removed, I was told all twelve nodes were clean. My oncologist said that I didn't need chemotherapy, but needed to start immediately on a six-week-long radiation treatment program. Many people see this as a very negative experience, but I actually didn't mind the weekly radiation treatments. I simply viewed them as burning away any cancer that was trying to grow back.

During the first few days of treatment, I noticed that the same women were there day after day. While we waited our turn for treatment, we struck up friendly conversations and soon began sharing our personal stories. We had all come from different walks of life and we each had unique stories about what had led us into similar treatment regimens. As the days passed, these women— eight of them to be exact—became much more than waiting room conversationalists. They became my support, my social life and, I dare say, a big part of my therapy, at least psychologically speaking. We shared everything with one other. Not just stories about our cancer, but stories of our families, our jobs, and our dreams. We named our little group the "Radiant Eight," and the office staff even came to know us by that name.

Janice, the first of the group to finish her treatment, continued visiting with us every week. It was hard for any of us to leave the group. I was the last one to finish, some three weeks later. Nonetheless, all eight of us still came together for my last appointment. It's pretty funny when you think about it. We were done with radiation and all pronounced free from cancer, but we just didn't want to say good-bye.

We decided that we would continue to meet twice a month to visit, just like some women meet to play cards, go bowling, or attend a Bible study. We always have enough to talk about to make the evening fly by. On the first meeting of each month, we have to report on our monthly breast self-exams. This great "buddy" system keeps us all accountable.

It has been more than three years since we first met at the hospital. To celebrate our anniversary each year, we all meet at one of our homes and throw ourselves a "Radiant Eight" dinner. *Everything* at the party is white—white tablecloths, napkins and decorations. We use white dishes and candles. We drink white wine and have gotten pretty creative at cooking dishes that are white, too (not just white rice and cottage cheese). We even dress in white.

The white color theme signifies, of course, that we are still clean from cancer, although I think it looks more like a little gathering of angels. Maybe that last thought isn't so far off. After all, these women *have been* angels to me.

Time for a Group Hug

My cancer survivor story doesn't involve help from one friend, but support and encouragement from an entire group, my breast cancer support group. They were special in many ways, but let me start at the beginning.

About nine years ago, a group of breast cancer survivors, most in their 30s and 40s, decided that our area needed a support group. With the assistance of a nurse, our local hospital, and the American Cancer Society, they started one. It met monthly at the hospital, using a conference room near the oncology unit. Eventually, about forty survivors were involved, with at least half of the ladies attending any given meeting.

A wonderful nurse, Brenda, handed me a flier about this group right after my surgery. At first, I wasn't interested in attending, feeling I could (or maybe should) handle recovery on my own. But as I struggled through my recovery, I decided it might be worth giving this group a try.

Long before the end of my first meeting, I was hooked. By sharing, I was able to release a number of emotions that I'd been keeping to myself for far too long—anxiety, self-pity and melancholy. Emotions of joy, hope, and laughter that had been scarce since my initial diagnosis were restored. And I also got the strength and courage I needed to continue on. It was really powerful. But what I remember most about the meeting was it ended with a big group hug.

My support group invited me to reacquaint myself with laughter.

They allowed me to share my feelings, helping me get through chemotherapy, follow-up testing, and more. We held one other up when, on rare occasion, we lost a member. I was inspired by guest speakers including therapists, surgeons, oncologists, beauticians, and dietitians. I took part in picnics, holiday dinner parties, and even a boat ride on a nearby lake, all with my husband at my side. But regardless of the location or activity, we always ended our time together with a big group hug.

It was such a simple act on Brenda's part, giving me a gentle nudge toward a support group, but it made a world of difference in my life. Although I was skeptical about being a part of this group at first, many of its members are among my best friends today. And when we're together, whether one-on-one or in a group, the last thing we still do before parting is give one another a big, warm hug.

It is more blessed to give than receive.

- Acts 20:35 -

Turkey Day

I was diagnosed with malignant melanoma in April of 1997. At the time, I didn't know anything about melanoma, the most deadly form of skin cancer. It's just not the kind of thing most 24-year-olds think about. Prior to the diagnosis, the only thing on my mind was moving. I'm a U.S. citizen, but had just accepted a new teaching assignment at a university in Montreal. My obvious concerns were getting the official paperwork completed and approved, finding housing in Montreal, packing my belongings, and getting from point A to point B.

My immediate reaction was not to go. I didn't want to leave my family, my friends, or my doctor, Dr. Jordan behind—especially with a cancer diagnosis. However, I'd already made a commitment to the school and knew that they were counting on me. In August I headed for Quebec. Dr. Jordan referred me to a college classmate of his, also a specialist in skin cancer, who had a practice in upstate New York about two hours from Montreal.

After moving to Canada, I had four surgeries in three months. In November, when I was well enough after the fourth surgery, I returned to Montreal to await the results of the biopsy. I was hardly thrilled at the prospect of needing yet another surgery. I was scared, tired, in pain from the surgery, and missing home terribly. I knew very few people and the ones I did know were my roommate's friends, so I didn't really count them as my own.

My family was hoping I would be well enough to come back to Iowa for Thanksgiving, but I was hardly able to get out of bed, let alone get on an airplane. I remember crying into my pillow Thanksgiving morning as I thought of the feast going on back home. No one was making a big turkey dinner that day in Canada. To them it was just another day. I thought about all my favorite foods and drifted off to sleep.

A few hours later, I was awakened by noise from the kitchen. Stephanie, my roommate, came in and asked if I was well enough to come to the dining room. Although in a lot of pain, I slowly got out of bed and put on my robe. The smell of food reached me long before I got to the door.

On the table was a veritable feast—turkey, stuffing, mashed potatoes and gravy, green beans, cranberry sauce, biscuits, and even pumpkin pie (very hard to find in French-Canadian Montreal)! In the kitchen, I saw one of my roommate's friends, someone I barely knew. Stephanie had told her that I greatly missed my family, so the two of them decided to prepare a traditional Thanksgiving dinner for me.

As I sat down to eat dinner with them, tears welled up in my eyes. I don't think I have ever been so touched in all my life Across Canada, while everyone else was doing their typical weekday activities, I was enjoying a home-cooked Thanksgiving dinner—just like they were back in Iowa.

Now, three years later, I'm cancer-free and on a mission to help educate people about melanoma. But I will never forget that incredible "Turkey Day" which allowed me to forget, even if only for an evening, my loneliness, fear, and pain.

Vacation Time

Most of us consider paid vacation as a requirement of any employment and count sick leave as a nice, but secondary, benefit. Having worked for the State of New Jersey for a number of years, I earned four weeks of paid vacation annually. I had also accumulated about three months of sick leave—not that I ever thought I would need it. Then came May 8, 1997, the day I was diagnosed with high-risk breast cancer.

As my doctor outlined the treatment program, my thoughts quickly turned to that vacation time and sick leave, and how important they would be to me now. He told me that my mastectomy would keep me off work for about six to eight weeks. With about four months of combined paid time off, I felt pretty comfortable about battling this disease without having to simultaneously worry about income and paying normal living expenses.

My attitude changed entirely in week four of the treatment program, when a lymph node sampling detected twenty-five positive (cancerous) nodes. My treatment program now expanded to four rounds of chemotherapy followed by a stem cell transplant and then radiation. As if that wasn't enough, my heart sank even further when I learned that it would be at least six more months before I could get back to work. How on earth could I ever continue to pay my day-to-day living expenses?

When I got home, I called Marjorie, my supervisor, to tell her about the new diagnosis and change in plans. I confided in her that I didn't know how I'd be able to make ends meet. She offered her sympathy and assured me that when I was physically able, I could return to a position in her department. I felt a little better about things, but still didn't know how I could make it through three months without pay.

The following week, my doorbell rang and to my surprise "Marj" and several other people were standing there holding some lovely floral arrangements and several helium-filled get-well balloons. Then Marj handed me a small, yellow envelope, the outside of which said simply "We Care!" The card inside, signed by about twenty-five of my co-workers, indicated that they wished me well and, as a small token of their support, had collectively donated enough of *their* vacation time and sick leave to fill in the three-month gap I was facing. I was speechless and grateful beyond description.

I wasn't aware until that moment that the State had a provision allowing co-workers to donate vacation time or sick leave for someone facing a catastrophic illness or injury. Even if I had known, I don't think I could have asked my co-workers to contribute. The neat part—thanks to Marj—was that I didn't have to ask. They cared about me enough to just do it.

Thank you ever so much!

*We can do
not great things—
only small things
with great love.*

- Mother Teresa -

What Could Be Cooler?

If there's anything most of us love to do, it's eat. We love picnics and barbecues. We love big potluck spreads at family reunions. And going out for dinner is always a welcome treat. There's no doubt about it, we just love food. So it's no surprise that food comes to the top of everyone's list when family or friends are in need. And I was definitely in need.

Two weeks earlier, my doctor had diagnosed my worst fear, breast cancer. I was to have an immediate mastectomy followed by a series of chemotherapy treatments. I was overwhelmed—physically, mentally, and spiritually. Needless to say, the last thing that my family or I felt like doing was preparing meals.

It took a while for the news to get around. But when it did, my family and friends came up with a novel solution to our food problem. They bought us a large, new cooler and set it on my front porch—sort of like the old milk box. Then on my chemo day and the two days that followed, they would deliver a complete dinner for me and my family.

They wanted to help, but they knew that I was feeling sick and were concerned that they might be bothersome. So they'd just put the meal into the cooler, often with a little note of encouragement, and slip away without a sound—like the fairy tale where little elves made shoes for the cobbler every night and then disappeared without a trace.

For maximum convenience, the food was packaged in disposable containers. No dishwashing and no containers for me to worry about returning to the right people. And boy, did we love the food! Whether it was macaroni and cheese or chicken cordon bleu, the love displayed by these actions was an incredible encouragement. I can't think of an easier way to help . . .

Ingredients
    1—large cooler
    Several disposable storage containers/bags
    Your culinary skills
    Food—your choice
    Love

Take any food of your choice. Prepare using your culinary skills. Place in disposable storage containers. Approximately one hour before dinnertime, deliver to residence and set carefully in cooler. Sprinkle generously with love.

Wiggin' Out

On New Year's Eve 1997, I was lying in my hospital bed recovering from the lumpectomy I just had. Before surgery I was told that if my lymph nodes tested negative for cancer, I wouldn't need chemotherapy. While I was still under the haze of anesthesia, the oncologist walked into my room. My comment was, "I don't need to see you; my nodes were clean." The oncologist smiled sadly and replied, "Not so fast; we have things to discuss."

Throughout my life I was always proud of my blond, straight hair. I wore my hair long, almost to my waist at times. The thought of losing all that hair to chemotherapy was hard to comprehend. But I was determined to rid myself of cancer, so chemo—and the consequent hair loss—was the price I would have to pay.

Real hair wigs are expensive, and doubly so when you want one with long hair. I wanted to appear as "normal" as possible and naturally gravitated to the long hair wig, but the one I wanted carried a price tag in excess of $625. The chemo proved to be very hard on my body and I could not work. As a result, money was tight and it seemed unreasonable to buy an expensive wig.

Lisa, a colleague from work, called to check on me one day. My fellow workers had been very supportive of my cancer treatment and had wanted to help as much as possible. There just didn't seem to be much they could do. Lisa knew I had planned to buy the wig and she asked me when she would get to see it. When I told her that I was not going to buy it because of the high price, she went to work rallying my co-workers.

They took up a collection of funds to purchase the wig for me and were able to raise $566 within a couple days. When I received the money, I was so moved by this display of care that it still brings tears to my eyes when I think of it. I felt a profound sense of gratitude for all the wonderful people in my life. Before I was diagnosed, I never realized how lucky I was to have so many wonderful friends who cared about what happened to me.

Because of their generosity, I was able to get the wig I wanted. Later that spring, I stood up in several family weddings. When I look at the pictures today, I see someone with a puffy chemo-face, but with hair looking as natural as it always had. When I wore my wig, people I interacted with didn't stare rudely at a hat or scarf knowing that I had no hair beneath. Many of them never knew.

It may seem vain to consider one's appearance when going through cancer treatment. And I often wondered if my vanity was excessive. I have since realized that during that time so much had been taken from me—my health, my ability to work, and my daily routines—to say nothing of the emotional toll. Looking like I had always looked was one of the few things I managed to retain.

Of all the gifts my colleagues gave me, this one was the best. It exemplified their deep concern and support for me. You see, the wig they gave me restored my confidence, not just my hair.

Wings of Light

It may not be the most glamorous job, but I love driving my big yellow school bus. Living in a rural community, most kids ride the bus, regardless of what grade they're in. For seventeen years I drove the bus, and it was a real treat for me be able to watch many of those kids grow up. While they seemed to change right before my eyes, I was oblivious to, or perhaps just in denial of, some changes in my own life. My biggest change occurred at the beginning of year 18 with the diagnosis of stage 4 breast cancer.

Perhaps the most disappointing thing was not being able to continue my daily routine of taking the kids to school and bringing them home again. I was simply too weak and with all the "Warning: Do Not Drive or Operate Equipment" drugs I was taking, I had to turn in my keys.

Initially, it was really tough. I live just two blocks from the elementary school on the main street that leads to it. We only have a dozen buses in our district, but every morning I would watch them drive by. Through the windows, I could see those energetic kids, "my kids," on their way to or from school. I missed them all so much.

About two weeks after I stopped driving, I watched bus #31, driven by Sherry (another long-time driver), begin the morning's routine progression—only I noticed something different this time. On the back of her bus hung a brightly lettered vinyl banner: "Ann's Wings of Light." I got all choked up. Then came Mary's bus, #9. She saw me standing at the window and gave a big wave.

As her bus passed, I saw that it, too, carried the sign. I had to reach for a tissue. In the next five minutes, ten more buses drove by, each proudly displaying the sign. I ran out of tissues, but not tears.

My co-workers must have been pointing out my home as they drove by because by the second or third day the kids were even waving to me out the windows or giving me the thumbs up sign. One of my favorite riders, Kristie, even made her own simple sign and held it up to the window as she rode by. It read: "Get Well—I Miss You, Kristie."

The banners remained intact from January through May, the end of the school year and the Relay for Life month in our state. We got special permission from the school board to drive one of the buses, emblazoned with all twelve signs and loaded with participants, to the event site. On the way, Mary handed out T-shirts to everyone that bore the same message: "Ann's Wings of Light." Although I was still recuperating and unable to run or walk at the time, I was thrilled to be able to go to the event and watch all my co-workers, friends, and even some of my students raise money in my honor for breast cancer awareness.

I wish I could adequately describe how wonderful those simple placards made me feel. They silently let me know that people were supporting me in my fight—my "wings" helped me fly at a time when I truly needed a lift.

Idea
Guide

Using This Book

One of the biggest challenges in putting together this book was trying to determine what order the stories should be in. There are a limitless number of ways this could be done, but I ultimately settled on the simplest way—alphabetical by title.

I regret, however, that doesn't provide you much guidance toward which ideas would best apply to your given circumstances and desires. In the interest of making this book more useful, I've included a table that categorizes the stories—first, by the general age of the support givers (children or adults), and then by the number of people involved [individuals (I), small groups (SG) or large groups (LG)].

The table indicates which category the original story was written in (•) and other categories it also applies to (•). There's really no right or wrong way to implement these ideas. Taking action, in almost any form, is the right thing to do.

I trust that you'll take the time to read every story. Each one has a special message and you may think of how to apply it in ways that I haven't thought of—so be creative! Tailor these ideas to fit your circumstances and those of your loved ones, whether they're facing cancer, AIDS, heart disease, giving birth, or just the chicken pox.

In most cases, all that's required of you is a little time and energy. The beauty of it is that this simple action may well be the single biggest encouragement your loved one receives. Next to their faith in God, it may also become a major source of internal strength as he or she faces the greatest physical challenge of their life.

In the final analysis, it's my belief that your expressions of love and support, in the form of *actions*, will be greatly treasured in the long run. One other thing—don't forget to have some fun with your efforts. It's often said that laughter is the best medicine, so be sure to laugh and smile and hug a little along the way.

KEY - I = individual   SG = small group   LG = large group
○ Could be applied   ● As written

	Children			Adults		
	I	SG	LG	I	SG	LG
A Rose of Hope	○	○	○	●	○	○
A Velvet Heart	○	○		●	○	
All Wrapped in Love		○	○	●	○	○
Angels Next Door				○	●	
Butch 'n Buster	○	○		●	○	
Can Do!			●			○
Circle of Friends		○			●	
Hand-in-Hand	○	●	○			
Hat Day			●			○
Hats and More Hats	○	●			○	○
I'm Going with You				●	○	
It Is a Joke	○	●	○			
It's for the Birds				●		
Just a Heartbeep Away					○	●
Just Say It!					●	
Life Goes On	○	○		●	○	
Making the Grade				●	○	

	Children			Adults		
	I	SG	LG	I	SG	LG
My Special Ally	●	●		●	●	
Net Working	●	●		●	●	
One Step at a Time	●	●		●	●	
Only a Call Away				●		
Out for a Joy Ride				●	●	
Paris in Springtime				●		
Pillow Buddy	●	●		●	●	
Queens of Hearts		●			●	
Ready, and—Action!	●	●		●	●	
School Spirit					●	●
Something Old . . .				●	●	
The Business of Caring						●
The Card's in the Mail	●	●		●	●	
The Chemo Pack	●	●		●	●	
The Great Shave-Off		●	●		●	●
The Green Room		●		●	●	
The Radiant Eight		●		●		
Time for a Group Hug		●		●		
Turkey Day				●	●	
Vacation Time					●	●
What Could Be Cooler?				●		
Wiggin' Out		●	●	●	●	●
Wings of Light					●	●

Resources

According to the American Cancer Society, approximately 1.22 million cases of cancer are diagnosed every year in the United States. We figure that's 1.22 million people who might benefit from some extra love and support.

If you want more information concerning cancer, please contact the following organizations:

American Cancer Society
> Website: www.cancer.org
> Phone: 800-ACS-2345
> Address: 1599 Clifton Rd NE, Atlanta, GA 30329

American Lung Association
> Website: www.lungusa.org
> Phone: 800-LUNG-USA
> Address: 1740 Broadway, New York, NY 10019

Cancer Care, Inc.
> Website: www.cancercare.org
> Phone: 800-813-HOPE
> Address: 1180 Ave of Americas, New York, NY 10036

Gynecologic Cancer Foundation
> Website: www.wcn.org/gcf/
> Phone: 800-444-4441
> Address: 401 N Michigan Ave, Chicago, IL 60611

National Alliance of Breast Cancer Organizations
> Website: www.nabco.org
> Phone: 610-668-1320
> Address: 9 E 27th St, 10th Floor, New York, NY 10016

National Cancer Institute
   Website: www.nci.nih.gov
   Phone: 800-4-CANCER
   Address: 31 Center Dr, Bethesda, MD 20892
National Cancer Prevention Fund
   Website:
   Phone: 800-249-0350
   Address: 1775 Sherman St #1845, Denver, CO 80203

National Cervical Cancer Coalition
   Website: www.nccc-online.org
   Phone: 818-909-3849
   Address: 16501 Sherman Wy #110, Van Nuys, CA 94106

National Ovarian Cancer Coalition
   Website: www.ovarian.org
   Phone: 888-OVARIAN
   Address: PO Box 4472, Boca Raton, FL 33429

Susan G. Komen Breast Cancer Foundation
   Website: www.komen.org
   Phone: 972-855-1600
   Address: 5005 LBJ Freeway #370, Dallas, TX 75244

Y-ME National Breast Cancer Organization
   Website: www.y-me.org
   Phone: 800-221-2141
   Address: 212 W Van Buren St, Chicago, IL 60607

For the early detection of cancer in people without symptoms: *Talk with you doctor*. Ask how these American Cancer Society guidelines relate to you.

AGE 18 to 39

Cancer-related checkup should be performed every three years. This should include the procedures listed below plus health counseling (such as tips on quitting tobacco use) and examinations for cancers of the thyroid, testicles, mouth, ovaries, skin, and lymph nodes. Some people are at higher risk for certain cancers and may need to have tests more frequently.

BREAST
Exam by a health care professional every three years. Self-exam every month.

UTERUS
Pelvic exam every one to three years with a Pap test.

CERVIX
Every woman who is, or has been, sexually active, or has reached age 18, should have an annual Pap test and pelvic examination. After three or more consecutive satisfactory normal annual examinations, the Pap test may be performed less frequently at the discretion of her physician.

AGE 40 & OVER

Cancer-related checkup should be performed every year. This should include the procedures listed below, plus health counseling and examinations for cancers of the thyroid, testicles, mouth, ovaries, skin, and lymph nodes. Some people are at higher risk for certain cancers and may need to have tests more frequently.

BREAST
Exam by a health care professional every year. Self-exam every month. Screening mammogram (breast X-ray) at age 40. Then every 1 to 2 years ages 40 to 49 and every year, age 50 and older.

UTERUS
Pelvic exam every year with a Pap test. Endometrial tissue sample at menopause, if at high risk.

CERVIX
Same as age 18 to 39

COLON & RECTUM
Digital rectal exam every year. Stool slide test every year after age 50. Sigmoidoscopy, preferably flexible, every 3 to 5 years after age 50.

PROSTATE
Annual digital rectal exam and prostate-specific antigen blood test should be performed every year beginning at age 50.

Remember: These guidelines are not rules and only apply to people without symptoms. If you have any doubts about whether you have cancer, see your doctor!

Bright Idea Award

Sara Sabalka, author of "I Didn't Know What To Do," has been recognized with a *Bright Idea Award* by the Colorado Women's Health Campaign (CWHC) for her idea to write and publish this book as part of an ongoing series.

On behalf of the CWHC, this award was presented by Mrs. Francene Owens, the First Lady of Colorado. The ceremony was held at the

*First Lady of Colorado
Mrs. Francene Owens and Sara*

Governor's mansion as part of the 1999 Colorado Women's Health Leadership Awards.

The CWHC is dedicated to raising awareness of disease prevention and health promotion for Colorado women between the ages of 45 and 65 through a coordinated state-wide voice for information, education, and advocacy. The Campaign educates women about the basic steps necessary to achieve better health, specifically in the areas of breast cancer, cardiovascular disease, osteoporosis, menopause and depression.

The *Bright Idea Award* recognizes individuals for offering an innovative health service for women and exemplifies the CWHC slogan, "Good Health for Women is Everyone's Business."

About the Author

Sara Sabalka is an outspoken advocate for the awareness and early detection of breast cancer. After her own diagnosis and lumpectomy in her late 20s, Sara went on to earn the title of "Ms. Colorado USA 1999." She then competed in the national pageant, where she placed in the top 10 and was recognized with the National Community Service Award.

Sara is on the National Speakers Bureaus of the American Cancer Society and the Susan G. Komen Breast Cancer Foundation. Since 1997, she has served on Komen's Special Events Committee for the Denver chapter. Sara received the BMW's Drive for the Cure "Heroine Award" in recognition of her volunteerism on behalf of breast cancer awareness.

In 1999, she was invited by Harpo Productions to run with "Team Oprah" in Milwaukee, Wisconsin's first-ever Race for the Cure. She has also been the subject of numerous television and print media stories.

Sara is a Colorado native where she lives with her family and dog "Buddy." She spends her free time enjoying all of the great activities Colorado has to offer.

Sara joins Team Oprah at Race for the Cure®

Share Your Story

Did someone do something special to provide hope, encouragement, and love to you during your battle with cancer or other difficult time in your life? Or do you know what someone did that was really special for a friend or family member? If so, we'd love to hear about it.

Please take a moment to jot down a few notes about the circumstances, what was done and how you felt touched by it. If you need more space, feel free to continue your story on additional pages. You're also welcome to submit your story through our website: **www.what-2-do.com**

OTHER TOPICS TO WRITE US ABOUT:
What-2-Do for Sick Kids
What-2-Do for Grieving Families
What-2-Do for Those with AIDS
What-2-Do for Caregivers

Your name:_____

Phone: (_____) _____-_____

E-mail address: _____@ _____

Your story:_____

_____

_____

_____

_____

_____

_____

_____

_____

_____

_____

_____

_____

_____

_____

_____

_____

By submitting your story, you agree that all or any portion of your story may be published by What-2-Do. You also agree that we may edit the content of any submittal. Finally, you agree that this is a "free will" submittal and that no compensation is being offered. What-2-Do agrees not to use your name without your written approval. If you do not agree with these terms, do not submit your story.

Mail to:

  What-2-Do, 8601 F-5 W Cross Dr #222, Littleton, CO 80123

E-mail to:

  www.what-2-do.com